THE WORLDS OF ARCHITECTURAL DIGEST

COUNTRY HOMES

THE WORLDS OF ARCHITECTURAL DIGEST

COUNTRY HOMES

EDITED BY PAIGE RENSE

EDITOR-IN-CHIEF, ARCHITECTURAL DIGEST

THE KNAPP PRESS   PUBLISHERS   LOS ANGELES

Published in the United States of America in 1982
The Knapp Press
5900 Wilshire Boulevard, Los Angeles, California 90036
Copyright © 1982 by Knapp Communications Corporation
All rights reserved
First Edition

Distributed by The Viking Press
625 Madison Avenue, New York, New York 10022

Distributed simultaneously in Canada by Penguin Books Canada Limited

Library of Congress Cataloging in Publication Data
Main entry under title: Country homes.
(The Worlds of Architectural digest)
Selected from Architectural digest.
1. Country homes. 2. Interior decoration.
I. Rense, Paige. II. Architectural digest
(Los Angeles, Calif.: 1925) III. Series.
NK2195.R87C6   1982   728.3'7   82-8989
                                         AACR2

ISBN 0-89535-102-1
Printed and bound in the United States of America

CONTENTS

FOREWORD

Who among us hasn't at one time or another fallen in love with a beautiful natural setting and imagined owning a country home there? It may have been a fantasy of a seaside cottage, a mountain retreat or an old stone house in some remote village.

For those who seek an alternative to the pressures and relentless pace of urban life, the country home offers a logical answer. But love, rather than logic, has inspired the residences selected for this volume. Each one represents an irresistible response on the part of its owner to a particular location, and the design of each is a solution to the challenge of creating a home in harmony with the surrounding landscape.

In choosing these nineteen country homes from the pages of ARCHITECTURAL DIGEST, one criterion has been variety. However, I think you'll find the characteristics they have in common equally interesting.

Almost without exception the owners of these country homes have created private worlds where they can pursue the activities they love best. It comes as no surprise to find that the outdoors plays a major role in many of their lives. The Govett family, for example, are ardent fishermen. The Norwegian log home they constructed in the Scottish Highlands is situated to afford them access to one of the finest fishing pools on the river Dee. Life at *Closeburn Stud,* an estate in Millbrook, New York, centers around the breeding of Thoroughbred horses and the owner's passion for racing, jumping and showing them.

"Sense of place" is a subject often explored in ARCHITECTURAL DIGEST, and the phrase takes on special meaning when applied to a country home. In this context it means that a residence must be integrated into its setting in a uniquely sensitive manner. The Swiss chalet of Robert Ricci, for instance, not only commands spectacular views of Alpine peaks, snow and sky, but is also a fresh interpretation of the traditional dwelling found in the surrounding countryside. The circular, conical-roofed structures that compose Jack Lenor Larsen's *Round House* were inspired by a Bantu compound. Yet they too are eminently suited to their landscape, a stretch of farmland in East Hampton, Long Island.

Several of the homes you'll encounter here were originally utilitarian structures—barns, stables, an old millhouse. Invariably their owners and designers cherish them for this reason, and in converting them took care to preserve their character.

It is frequently the ideal of a simpler life that attracts people to the country. As you visit the homes in this volume of THE WORLDS OF ARCHITECTURAL DIGEST, I think you'll agree with me that simplicity can provide the wellspring for an immensely vital approach to life—and to design.

Paige Rense
Editor-in-Chief
Los Angeles, California

THE WORLDS OF ARCHITECTURAL DIGEST

COUNTRY HOMES

ROCKY MOUNTAIN RETREAT

High in the Colorado mountains, where elk and bighorn sheep roam and lupine grows wild in sunny openings between clumps of lodgepole pine, there is a cabin that has stood for more than six decades. Built on land that was once a gold claim, it was at first little more than a shelter against the winter snows and the crisp winds that blow down the mountain slopes in early spring. Later it served as a summer home for Mr. and Mrs. Perkins Sams and their growing family. Then, with grown children and grandchildren, they decided to make extensive changes—partly for their own comfort, partly as the starting point for a complex of cabins to accommodate family and friends comfortably.

Although remodeling primarily involved restructuring and enlarging, they called upon Joseph Minton, of Fort Worth, Texas, their friend and interior designer of long standing, to guide the project from the beginning. "There were many people involved here," says Mr. Minton. "There was a builder who had grown up in the area and knew the peculiarities of the climate and materials. There was a mason who spent six months finding stones for the fireplace and putting them in place. The workmen were all local, fine craftsmen." The builder used many traditional methods from early Colorado days. Mrs. Sams explains: "Whenever he spotted a tree that he thought would be good for a cabin, he'd ring it and leave it to stand for three or four years to 'kill dry.' That way it wouldn't warp, as it would if it were felled and left on the ground to dry."

Construction started in September and went through July. As the building progressed, plans were sometimes changed. "Nearly every week," says Mr. Minton, "we'd have three-way conversations—between the Samses, the builder and myself. The fireplace wall was moved from where it was originally planned. Even the placement of the windows was changed. Originally there was a space calling for a wall, but we looked up at the gorgeous mountain and decided to leave it open." Much of the design is integral to the construction. The builder often went out to look for trim and returned with a truckload of pieces to make moldings, joists, braces, handles, windows. Drawer pulls came from bent twigs, and the cabin itself from lodgepole pine growing on the property. It is a house for people who clearly love the country. Perkins Sams says: "Anything you do to your home is insignificant compared to the outdoors." Nevertheless, the interior had its demands. "It is a house that puts you in touch with the integrity of materials," says the designer. "I wanted that feeling throughout, and also the house needed a feeling of warmth. I used many country antiques from France, England and America."

Appropriateness to location and the needs of the owners are Joseph Minton's design criteria. "Joe takes me seriously when I say this room has to take a lot of hard wear, and I don't want to worry about maintenance," says Mrs. Sams. "He knows I like rooms to have a casual feeling, so they can easily accommodate new things. He knows Perkins likes to cook and wanted commercial equipment at one end of the kitchen. We have a cool closet for things you don't want to refrigerate but that need to be kept cold, like freshly caught fish. At four o'clock Perkins can say, 'We'll have fish for dinner tonight,' and go out to the lake. And I *know* we won't be eating scrambled eggs!" In keeping with the country—the fragrance of the trees after a rain, the stillness of the forest broken by the call of a mountain jay, the thrust of wind through aspen and pine—Joseph Minton has created a cabin of uncommon charm in the splendid and rugged mountains of Colorado.

PRECEDING PAGE: *Nestled against a hillside in the Rocky Mountains of Colorado, the log cabin retreat of Mr. and Mrs. Perkins Sams was restructured and enlarged under the guidance of designer Joseph Minton.* OPPOSITE: *Indigenous materials were used throughout the home, as in the Living Room, where a stone fireplace anchors beams of lodgepole pine. Forming a congenial area for conversation are a country settee and commodious chairs.* ABOVE: *In the Dining Area, two tables permit dining flexibility, with Windsor chairs surrounding the table in the background. Kilim rugs warm the brick and oak parquet flooring.*

5

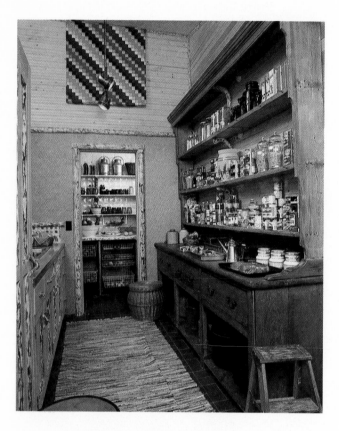 

ABOVE: *In the Pantry, cabinet handles and drawer pulls were fashioned from pine twigs, and moldings from split logs. Hewing to the country spirit, an antique pine dresser provides storage space.* ABOVE RIGHT: *A Kitchen window frames a view of the lake.* OPPOSITE: *In the Master Bedroom, the detailing of ceiling beams and bay window exhibits the inventive craftsmanship that distinguishes the cabin. The patchwork-quilt-patterned bedcovering, window seat upholstery and draperies complement the cheerful small-scale floral wall fabric and the rug.*

CONVERTED CARRIAGE HOUSE

Some people spend their lives falling in love with dilapidated barns or drafty houseboats or broken-down windmills. To them, taking a building most people would dismiss as unlivable and transforming it into a home of style and character becomes an irresistible challenge. When designer Edith Bain decided to move out of New York City, no stout country Tudor or rustic shingled saltbox could compare with an old stable set on the edge of an estate overlooking the Hudson Valley, designed by the great architectural firm of McKim, Mead & White. "Originally, the first floor of the stable housed carriages, equipment for horses and a supply room for the veterinarian," explains Mrs. Bain. "Upstairs, there was a small kitchen and a few bedrooms; this was where groundsmen lived at the time the original owners built the estate, seventy years ago."

Instead of making drastic architectural changes, Mrs. Bain decided to restore the existing weathered wood and brick and keep as much of the original layout as possible. On the first floor, the main room, where carriages had been kept, became the living room and dining area. The veterinarian's room converted easily into a kitchen, and the tack room is now a study. Throughout the house the designer preserved the uniqueness and history of the building. Wicker furniture was chosen to avoid detracting from the brick walls, the herringbone-patterned floors and the large curved windows. Because the study had been a tack room, the old stable gear was left hanging on the walls, and Mrs. Bain keeps this room filled with interesting and unusual artifacts. "I constantly find new treasures, and I delight in changing things completely around," she says.

Another unusual feature—and a constant reminder that the house was originally a stable—is an exposed drain, a necessity in the days when carriages and stable floors needed to be washed off. Mrs. Bain purposely placed her dining room table right over the drain. "I always tease my guests. I tell them if my cooking is really bad they can dispose of their meal the second I turn my back." A lively imagination and keen sense of humor, coupled with a genuine love and respect for historic architecture, are seen everywhere. Upstairs Mrs. Bain has turned what was the small kitchen into a bath and dressing area, keeping the veterinarian's stone sink.

The designer made all three bedrooms identical: An antique iron and brass bed is set at an angle in the middle of each room; bamboo blinds shade the windows; and a plant and a pair of wicker stools are beside every bed. "I wanted the beds to dominate the rooms in every way possible. In addition, it is very important, in a house like this, to be able to see empty corners and antique radiators. In fact, when I first moved in, there were no radiators at all on the first floor. Instead of installing modern ones, I literally spent months scouring the countryside in an effort to find old radiators. That's why I treat them almost like sculpture."

It is always instructive to see how interior designers choose to decorate their own homes. "When I moved out of New York, I not only cleared out my closets, I cleared out my life," says Mrs. Bain. "I pared down my possessions and kept only what was really essential. It seems like a more sensible way to live. Even with my clients, I prefer not to buy new things but to work with what someone has. While few of my designs are as stark as this one, I do believe in simplicity and order. I think one of the reasons people get confused today is because they have too many things around—too many tables to put things on, too many drawers and closets to stuff things into. I keep life simple. It's a lot more fun."

PRECEDING PAGE: *Inspired by the architectural detailing and historical resonance of a stable on the grounds of a Hudson Valley estate, designer Edith Bain converted it into a home for herself.*

ABOVE: *Like the turn-of-the-century manor house it served, the stable was built by the architectural firm of McKim, Mead & White. In modifying the structure, a smaller front entrance was installed within the chevron-paneled sliding door.*

Herringbone-patterned brick flooring enlivens the Entrance Hall, which opens to the kitchen, at left, once a veterinarian's supply room, and the stalls where horses were kept. Iron grillwork gives a harplike grace to the wooden partitions.

BELOW: *The spacious sweep of the Living Room, where carriages were housed, sets off the varied brickwork and the stately beamed oak ceiling.*

RIGHT: *Underscoring the beauty of the setting, casual furnishings, in unobtrusive wicker and rattan, form a conversation area. An arched window, framed in wood, creates a naturalistic panel above an antique radiator enclosed by a brass railing. "I wanted to be able to look out the window undisturbed by harsh colors, fancy fabric or crowded walls," Mrs. Bain says.*

OPPOSITE ABOVE: *Valuing the sculptural beauty of the iron hooks that once held saddles, bridles and reins, the designer retained them on the oak-paneled walls of the Study, formerly the tack room.* OPPOSITE LEFT: *Faithful to the spirit of her home, Mrs. Bain fitted the Kitchen with walnut cabinets; their tongue-and-groove construction echoes that of the original woodwork.* OPPOSITE RIGHT: *Wicker chairs and a glass and steel table constitute an informal ensemble in the Dining Area.* ABOVE: *Placed on the diagonal, the antique iron and brass bed assumes aesthetic prominence within the minimalism of the Bedroom.*

ALPINE CHALET

Whenever he feels the pressures of city life closing in on him, or when the demands of business become too strong, Robert Ricci, founder and president of the fashion house of Nina Ricci, flees Paris for his chalet in the Swiss Alpine hamlet of Klosters. The picturesqueness of the small village and its mountain setting cannot be exaggerated. Imagine a sunny morning in January, just after a heavy snowfall has transformed the landscape into a snowscape, coating with white even the smallest twigs on the trees. It is a marvelous day for skiing and Mr. Ricci, looking well pleased with life, sits on the balcony of his chalet enjoying the warmth of the sun. He speaks of his attachment for this lovely part of the world: "Long before I built this house, I discovered Klosters. That was when my children were small and we came here for their holidays, living in a hotel. After a few years, I rented a chalet, and we came more often. Finally, I felt that I wanted a place of my own, so I designed this with the help of the late Georges Geffroy, who was a friend of mine."

The building site, which is on high ground slightly above the village, was chosen for its stupendous view of the Alpine peaks, the forest and the sky. The chalet—with its broad eaves, wooden sun balcony and painted shutters—at first glance resembles the typical Grisons house. The Grisons, forming the central link of the great Alpine chain, comprise about one sixth of the total area of Switzerland and join the frontiers of Austria and Italy. Naturally Robert Ricci made every effort to conform to the Grisons style. Yet, on closer inspection, it becomes apparent that he and his architect took certain liberties with the classic Grisons chalet plan. For one thing, instead of installing the usual small casement windows, they opened large windows in several rooms to let the outside in, making them of double glass to keep out the winter's cold. And contrary to local custom, the chalet's rooms are of ample size. But the greatest surprise is the gracefully curving stairway that spirals upward, dividing the living room from the dining room with drama and flair.

Robert Ricci is a perfectionist. He has applied to the task of building his chalet the same rigorous standards that he uses in the creation of a gown or a perfume. The ceiling of the entrance hall, for example, is intricately inlaid with small fan-shaped pieces of Arolla pine, the native wood used throughout the house. The mosaic of tiles on the first floor was made by combining terra-cotta hexagons with white marble triangles. All these ancient techniques are fast disappearing, even in eastern Switzerland. The living room ceiling is coffered—but with a difference. Arolla pine forms the crossbeams, which are superimposed on a white plastic base. The fireplace wall of unadorned white marble, the antique Chinese rug, and the wallcovering and draperies of Thai silk provide an understated background for two important antiques: a carved pine bridal chest from the eighteenth century and a painted Grisons armoire. The dining room doubles as a library. Here two adjacent walls are joined by a curved section filled by a suede banquette, bookshelves and a center niche. This is flanked at either end by floor-to-ceiling cabinets painted in the antique style of the district. Georges Geffroy designed the pedestal dining table and chairs, as well as the tall bronze torchères that light the room so beautifully.

It is clear that Robert Ricci loves perfection of design. Generosity and a love of nature also are typical of him—and all of these qualities are evident in his chalet at Klosters. The words of his chauffeur, Pierre, can stand as a summary of Robert Ricci: "M. Ricci n'est pas un monsieur. Il est un seigneur."

PRECEDING PAGE: *The Swiss village of Klosters is the setting for Robert Ricci's home—an adaptation of the classic Alpine chalet.* ABOVE: *Boldly patterned suede-upholstered entrance hall doors open to reveal the intricately painted panels of an 18th-century armoire in the Living Room.*

18

French architect Georges Geffroy, who collaborated with Mr. Ricci on the plan of the chalet, designed the graceful staircase. Plants adorn the Entrance Hall, providing uninhibited contrast to the terra-cotta and marble tile floor.

OPPOSITE ABOVE: *The Living Room ceiling, coffered in native Arolla pine, echoes the tiled floor in both form and color. Thai-silk-covered walls and an unornamented expanse of marble around the fireplace create a clear interlude between those strong architectural elements. A Grisons peasant's chair of carved wood recalls the local heritage.*
OPPOSITE AND ABOVE: *Georges Geffroy designed the pedestal table and Neo-Classically inspired chairs in the Dining Room. Painted cabinets employ antique Grisons designs.*

ABOVE: *Reproduced from an antique French fabric, the Provincial cotton used extensively in the Guest Suite radiates a country spirit. The sofa is served by oval pine tables designed by Mr. Ricci. Bookshelves made of Arolla pine, a consistent architectural element throughout the residence, flank the marble fireplace. In the adjacent sleeping alcove, walls are covered in Thai silk.* OPPOSITE: *Alpine summits and snow-laden pines are visible from the Master Suite.*

A SPANISH COUNTRY VILLA

Extremadura, a region of western Spain comprising the provinces of Cáceres and Badajoz, lies along the Portuguese border. It is an area resonant with history, and much of the countryside and many of the towns are filled with ancient towers and palaces and large rambling houses with façades emblazoned with heraldic devices. Some of the buildings date from Roman times, others from the Gothic, the Renaissance and the Baroque. One of the most interesting towns in the region is Trujillo, some 150 miles southwest of Madrid, beyond Toledo and Ciudad Real. Lying at the foot of the Sierra de Guadalupe, the ancient town—as well as the surrounding countryside—is famous as the birthplace of many of the conquistadores who sailed from Spain in the sixteenth century to discover the riches of North and South America and the Caribbean. In fact, the palace built by Francisco Pizarro, the conquerer of Peru, is on the main plaza of Trujillo.

In recent years, many Spaniards and others from every part of the world have been attracted by the ancient town and have come in search of country houses, and in the process some of the old buildings and the palaces have been beautifully restored. These enthusiasts have come to be called the "Friends of Trujillo," and one of the first among them was interior designer Duarte Pinto Coelho. He, too, wanted a house for himself in the area, and he soon found an appropriate *finca*, a country estate located near the town, in an enchanted setting filled with ancient oaks. He knew it would provide a welcome relief from the urban pressures of Madrid, where he has an apartment, to take up the life of a gentleman farmer near Trujillo, when time permitted. The designer achieved his goal with characteristic speed and enthusiasm. He soon had a respectable collection of cows, horses and dogs and he indulged

in irrigation projects, building reservoirs and small aqueducts. Naturally he built a big house with numerous guest rooms for his many friends.

In creating the house, Señor Pinto Coelho brought into play all his ideas and talents as a professional interior designer. Portuguese by birth, he lived for many years in Paris as a young man, and then began to spend a good deal of time in Spain as well. Finally he decided to settle in Madrid, and later brought all his intensity and experience to the design of his country home in Trujillo. "The first thing I had to do," Señor Pinto Coelho explains, "was to make certain that the house conformed to this particular region of Spain. I wanted to give the impression that it had always been here. Next were the obvious elements of comfort: livability, enough space."

The completed house—indeed, it does look as if it has stood on the land for many generations—consists of a central part with two floors, an adjoining service wing, a patio and a swimming pool with pavilion. The approach is a reflection of the designer's simple but firm belief that houses are "to be lived in." Certainly one of the most graceful and comfortable rooms in the home is the dining room/kitchen. There is little doubt that it is the perfect illustration of the designer's guiding principle that comfort and hospitality and livability are all-important. The room looks out over a patio, and the atmosphere is in every possible way warm, rustic and *simpático*.

Easy enough to understand is Duarte Pinto Coelho's enthusiasm for country life and for the region of Extremadura. Indeed, he projects the definite feeling that this has always been his life. The house he made for himself in Trujillo gives an immediate sense of permanency, an impression that derives from more than his talent. It also derives from his devotion to his friends and his enthusiasm for life.

*In building his country villa in the Spanish town of
Trujillo, designer Duarte Pinto Coelho served as his own
architect.* PRECEDING PAGE: *Stone chips covering the façade are
native to Spain's Extremadura region.* ABOVE AND OPPOSITE
BELOW: *The 18th-century Chinese wallpaper in the Living
Room once graced the home of Sir Walter Scott. Printed
cotton upholstery fabric, multihued Indian pillows and
kilim rugs intensify the sense of abundance. Indo-Portu-
guese tables with ivory inlay add pointillistic sparkle.*

TOP: *Wrought by prisoners of the Napoleonic wars, a collection of* paille *marquetry objects in the Living Room forms a poignant link to the past.* FOLLOWING PAGES: *Inimitably cheerful, the rustic Dining Room/Kitchen is enhanced by a beamed ceiling, indoor shutters and tile architraves. Blue and white tableware and informal floral centerpieces further the relaxed mood. A 1920s painting offers a visual pun on dining.*

A collection of Neapolitan gouaches, many of them im-
mortalizing the pyrotechnics of Mt. Vesuvius, provides a
graphic background in the Master Bedroom. Eighteenth-
century fabric reinforces the historical tenor and comple-
ments the related pattern of a point d'Hongrie rug.

TOP: *Other views of Naples line the walls of the Master Bath. Persian rugs and a gilt bamboo settee add inviting comfort.* ABOVE: *Around the swimming pool, urns and finials embellish the native stone detailing of the walls and pavilion.*

GRACIOUS OXFORDSHIRE COACH HOUSE

She could be called a legend, but Nancy Lancaster would not like the definition. She would ask for privacy—even anonymity—and she is happy simply pruning her roses and living quietly in Oxfordshire. What she may not fully realize is that the rooms she and John Fowler decorated together during the decades following World War II still set standards in England, and the word *elegance* is associated clearly with her name. Her modesty is genuine, but it is misplaced. After all, she never even put her name to the decorating firm of Colefax & Fowler. It was a collaboration of pyrotechnics and common sense, sheer talent and good times, blazing rows and firm friendship—and it influenced an entire generation.

She lives much of the time now on the grounds of her former home, *Haseley Court*, in a cottage she calls *Coach House*—the name is a euphemism for "cart shed"; it had a mud floor and no windows and was not even grand enough for the carriages before she converted it to its present state twenty-five years ago. She lived here while the big house was being decorated, then lent it to a steady stream of grateful friends. The rooms are small and, as Mrs. Lancaster observes, if more than four people are in the dining room "they have to sit on each other's laps." The rooms are deliberately modest, for she sold her magnificent furniture when she sold Haseley Court. She took only a few things, such as her famous pair of Elizabethan portraits, to her London apartment, where she felt they would be more at home in the grand space of Wyatville's former studio. "There's no point in carrying things around with you just because you have them," she says. "I won't put Chippendale mirrors in this room with no cornice. That would be like having pearls in a pigsty."

This kind of suitability was the criterion Mrs. Lancaster always used for her grand houses, and it is as pertinent here. "You could say I have a sense of what a house needs," she says. "I simply get a feeling for the personality of a house or garden. In everything, you want to understate; don't do everything to the last detail. Let other people's imagination work." Such a point of view is not far from that particularly English genius for rooms that, to the unknowing, look as though the interior design had not yet begun. It is a deliberate courting of the old, a feeling that a few worn edges and a little dust soften things in just the right way. Certainly some of Mrs. Lancaster's most successful rooms have been those where her work showed the least. She has made colors look like part of the old plaster rather than applied pigment, and she loves subtly faded fabrics. Her own flat in London she decorated twenty-five years ago, and it has never been changed. There is no need, for it was right the first time.

Perhaps it is unusual that anyone born in America should understand English rooms so well. However, Nancy Lancaster does come from Virginia; she is devoted to her birthplace and returns to the state twice a year, to savor the spring and the autumn and to advise on the restoration of *Stratford Hall* for the Robert E. Lee Memorial Foundation. But Mrs. Lancaster is not inclined to be nostalgic. Her gardening feet are planted firmly on today's ground. The beautiful houses she has lived in have all changed hands, but she can say, without a trace of regret: "Anything I've ever done is gone, but I have no cause for complaint. I've always loved houses and gardens, and fortunately I've been lucky enough to have lived in some beautiful ones. So many people love beautiful places just as much as I do, and have to live in hideous ones. I've been able to afford luxury, and I had a good run for my money. It isn't *Gone with the Wind*, you know. It's only the 'End of the Breeze.'"

Nancy Lancaster, long a major influence in English interior design, now lives in Coach House, on her former Oxfordshire estate, Haseley Court.
PRECEDING PAGE: *The 14th-century barn stands behind the garden that Mrs. Lancaster planted over twenty-five years ago and still enjoys tending.*

RIGHT: *The brewhouse, surmounted by a clock tower, was built in 1754; the laundry (right) dates from 1750.*

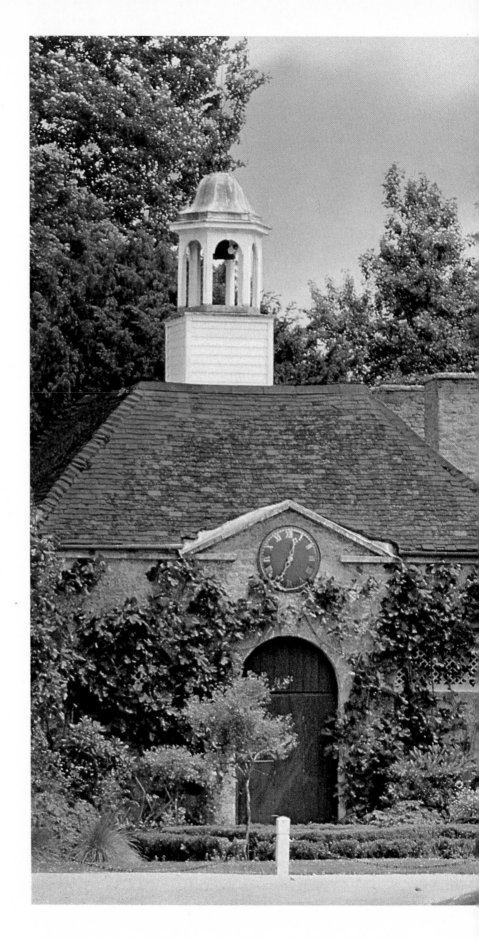

34

ABOVE: *Mrs. Lancaster, recognized as a doyenne of casual elegance, explains the deliberately modest appointments of the Sitting Room: "I won't put Chippendale mirrors in this room with no cornice." Cool color unifies an authoritative mixture of elements, including cotton slipcovers, delft porcelain objects and narrow painted lines that hint of a cornice. Amid a profusion of artworks are architectural views by Jan Kip.* OPPOSITE ABOVE: *A sleigh chair affords jaunty repose in the Sitting Room.* OPPOSITE: *Trompe l'oeil paneling lends formality to the small Dining Room; slipcovers provide casual contrast. Adding diversity are an antique French commode, an English mirror and a bold rug.*

ABOVE: *A Guest Room wrapped in floral-printed wall-paper and cotton fabric brings the garden atmosphere indoors. The painted beds were retained from a former residence, Ditchley Park. A botanical study amplifies the theme.* OPPOSITE: *The subtle hues that Mrs. Lancaster calls "no colors" enhance the unaffected simplicity of the Master Bedroom. Anchored by the strong, dark lines of an American cherrywood bed, the wallpaper, fabrics and rug contribute a gentle interplay of patterns. Sporting prints and a group of silhouettes represent facets of English artistry.*

Allowing nature to rule the garden, Nancy Lancaster says:
"I like gardens to have an architectural feel and formality,
a definite design on the grandest possible scale. Then I
throw that away; hide it with roses, vines, even ivy; let it
run wild; let flowers take charge." ABOVE: Sweet rocket and
roses perfume an informal border. OPPOSITE ABOVE: Weep-
ing mulberries cascade within a boxwood maze patterned
after a Roman church floor. OPPOSITE LEFT: A small garden
bench was copied from an 18th-century design. OPPOSITE
RIGHT: Hibiscus and datura emblazon a garden wall.

ECHOES OF AFRICA

When designer Jack Lenor Larsen decided in the early 1960s to build a house for himself in a style more familiar to the Bantu tribesmen of Africa south of the Congo than to the inhabitants of the Long Island village of East Hampton, where he had bought a tract of farmland, his friends were neither surprised nor scandalized. Knowing this remarkable man—weaver, traveler, teacher and textile authority—and knowing that his life and work are inseparable, they found it altogether natural that he should adapt a form of architecture deriving from one of the cultures that have inspired him to champion formerly neglected handicrafts and to spearhead a revolution in fabric design and its production.

Mr. Larsen recalls the origins of the house: "By 1961 I was reacting against glass-house dwellings. I wanted a country house, but one without suburban connotations. On a visit to Africa I had particularly liked the pattern of several small separate circular rooms forming a horseshoe, characteristic of the Ndebele villages near Pretoria. Their design struck me as handsome and reasonable." The late architect Robert Rosenberg drew plans for the house from a model by Mr. Larsen. Construction took one year to plan, and two more to complete. The mud walls and thatched roofs of the Bantu original could not be duplicated on Long Island. Instead, the walls of the first two rooms to be built—the main house and the guest house—were made of poured concrete, with two layers of steel and a rough plaster surface. And the roofs were made of cedar shakes stacked in depth to thicken them at the edges, a refinement current among the Indians of the American Northwest.

Under the conical roofs, the radiating beams of the ceiling are of rough-sawn fir. Floors are of blue-stone flag or unglazed Mexican tile. Many of the essential fixtures, including stoneware bathroom conveniences and baked-clay light switches, are handcrafted. Furniture ranges from chiefs' chairs of handcut wood to a Saarinen pedestal table, and leather armchairs and sofas designed by Benjamin Baldwin. Countless ethnic artifacts and objects from the owner's private collection—which includes several thousand examples of antique and modern textiles from Africa and Afghanistan, from Java and Peru—contribute to the extraordinary ambience of the residence. They are constantly being replaced by other objects from his collection, as the spirit moves him, and, in the words of a close friend and associate: "The *Round House* reflects Jack's endless travels and his genuinely 'global' nature. Like him, the house and the garden are never at all static or dull."

From the outset, the house was designed to include the normal quota of civilized amenities. Over the course of time, Mr. Larsen has supplemented these, most notably by his addition of a glass and acrylic conservatory along the perimeter of the main house that faces the garden. The conservatory brings more light into the living area at the center, and it provides space for a sunken whirlpool spa. At present the studio, from which the loom has gone, serves as a summer living room for both host and guests. It is, however, still used as a study by Mr. Larsen when he is busy preparing a new collection for his New York showrooms or writing one of his books on weaving, dyeing or fabric-making.

Snugly placed among groves of tall bamboo, sheltered by well-tended native trees, linked to its environment by curving walls and circular gardens, the Round House is perfectly at ease in its Long Island setting. "I would gladly fly back from Bombay simply to be able to spend the weekend at home in East Hampton," says Jack Lenor Larsen. And it would be extremely difficult to disagree with him.

For his unconventional East Hampton country home, Jack
Lenor Larsen created, in microcosm, his own version of an
African village. The noted textile designer built a complex
called the Round House, which takes its inspiration from
Bantu compounds of thatched-roof mud huts. PRECEDING
PAGE: *Along the gardenside perimeter of the main house,
Mr. Larsen added a redwood, glass and acrylic conservatory.* ABOVE: *In the Conservatory, a Turkoman rug provides a lively background for bentwood chairs and a slate-
topped table.* OPPOSITE: *Under a whorl of fir beams, African
objects fill the bluestone-floored Living Room of the main
house. The ceramic fireplace is by Karen Karnes.*

OPPOSITE: *The Studio, once the designer's weaving work-room, now functions as an airy summer living room. Fir beams and reed fencing overhead complement the primitive appeal of royal Congolese chairs brought from Africa, Thai baskets and Mexican tile flooring.* ABOVE LEFT: *A small Guest Room is surfaced in rough-sawn wood and suede. The pastel drawing is by John Opper.* ABOVE: *In the Master Bath, primitive patterns are reinterpreted in Erik Erikson's stained glass window. The stoneware vanity appointment by Karen Karnes is as much sculpture as fixture.*

The main house and the guest house were constructed of cedar shakes and reinforced concrete. The circular wall of the studio was erected by using the wood forms employed originally in shaping the concrete. Luxuriant planting integrates the residence with its environment.

IN ANCIENT PEDRAZA

The vivid colors, strong lines and occasional sumptuousness familiar to admirers of the work of Paco Muñoz are curiously missing from his country home at Pedraza. Their absence is, of course, intentional. Paco Muñoz, one of Spain's leading interior designers, is concerned with congruity, with the need to create a décor conforming to locale. Pedraza is a small seventeenth-century village perched on a hilltop near Segovia, in central Spain. It shares a spectacular site with the castle of its former ducal owners, the battlements now crumbled. The plaza is cobbled, the surrounding houses arcaded. The brownstone of which they are built is, even in winter, warm to the eye and the heart. Here, more than twenty years ago, in *La Casona*, Paco Muñoz found his country retreat. From five derelict farm buildings he created a spacious and understated residence to suit his needs: to escape the pressures of his hectic life in Madrid and to design in peace.

The expansive home he made was also intended to satisfy two other important aims: to respect the intimacy and dignity of the old village and to provide a country house that was comfortable but not ostentatious. The lofty living room, formerly the old barn, is on two levels. Its main floor leads to the garden, from which there are views over the bare plateau separating Pedraza from the mountains overlooking Madrid. Furnished informally, the room gives a feeling of spacious ease. The dining room is more intimate. Here, beneath a low beamed ceiling, wooden chests and chairs and a wide white stone fireplace are complemented by embroidered chair coverings and warm-hued fabrics. The effect is welcoming, and immensely appropriate to the quiet country life that is the essence of old Pedraza.

There is much to delight the eye. Paco Muñoz is also a collector, one of unusual and often witty taste.

Consider the brass eagle lecterns, for example, that are boldly clamped to the living room balustrade. More functional are the magnificent cupboards and chests, and the tester beds from the royal palace of *La Granja*. There are numerous sculptures, including a second-century Roman stone torso, many paintings and much fine pewter. The pewter, designed by Señor Muñoz, is made in the Pedraza factory he set up to provide local employment. His hand is evident also in the elegant octagonal white dinner service. In addition to these, Paco Muñoz designs a host of fabrics, furniture, leather and metalwork, as well as supervising the factories where they are made.

The visitor looking for the source of inspiration behind this varied output need not look far. It will be found in the designer's private art gallery. Converted from three old cottages that stood beside his house, the gallery holds what is more than just a personal collection. For many years, until Generalísimo Franco died, in fact, it was not prudent for Abstract artists to practice in Spain. Thus, the work of native sculptors and painters such as Chillida, Tapiès, Viola and other leaders of the Modern movement were almost unknown in their own country. The collection that Paco Muñoz assembled, but could not exhibit, contains some notable treasures, all officially proscribed. But what they had to say was transmitted covertly by Señor Muñoz, by way of his designs, to every corner of Spain and far beyond. The ban has since been lifted, and the work of these artists can now be freely enjoyed.

The example Paco Muñoz set by refurbishing La Casona in a fashion so faithful to the character of ancient Pedraza was such that those who followed him and helped to breathe new life into the village have emulated his reticence. The result is an entrancing and intelligent example of urban conservation.

OPPOSITE: *Post-and-beam construction preserves the rusticity of the Living Room. The balcony is appointed with a Catalan model of a horse-drawn coach and a 19th-century French dogcart.* BELOW: *In the Dining Room, antique carved wood chairs and an open hearth extend the warm traditional mode. The pewter soup tureen and candlesticks on the table were manufactured in the Pedraza factory established by Sr. Muñoz to stimulate local employment.*

OPPOSITE: *Both functional and fanciful are the pair of opulently draped, crown-surmounted tester beds that distinguish the principal Guest Room.* BELOW: *The versatile Master Bedroom doubles as a sitting room. The sculptures on the glass-topped table are by José Luis Sanchez and José Maria de Labra Suazo. A gilt-framed Spanish Hussar jacket is displayed above the mantel. The sleeping area is dominated by a Portuguese bed with turned wood posts.*

Paco Muñoz houses his collection of contemporary Spanish art in the Gallery next to the house. OPPOSITE: *Aged wood beams set off paintings and sculpture. Artworks, left to right, are by Oteiza, Tapiès, two by Pablo Palazuelo, and Chillida.* BELOW: *Pottery by Artigas and paintings by Manolo Mompó and Manolo Millares enrich a seating area.*

BELOW: *Created from several old farm buildings, the residence and art gallery are faithful to the historic character of the village.* OPPOSITE: *An arched carriageway leads from the cobblestone plaza to the front entrance of La Casona.*

RURAL MEDLEY

When a New York doctor and art collector first saw a group of dilapidated outbuildings that had once formed part of an estate in the Hudson Valley, he was reminded of the farm his family had owned in Norway. This memory was enough to make him stop and take notice of something that most country house-hunters would have dismissed as a jumble of formerly utilitarian constructions: an icehouse that was little more than a weathered wooden cube; an imposing but ruined greenhouse, attached to a small cottage; a root cellar and two other large plain sheds. But the group of buildings spoke to him as stray houses sometimes do: "Take me in. Make something marvelous of me." The setting was beautiful—an area of farms and estates, with an occasional Rhenish "castle" on the heights overlooking the Hudson. The buildings were cut off from what had been the main house and were isolated in a clearing surrounded by woods. A large pond fed by a mountain stream had been "put in" next to the icehouse.

The new owner showed the place to an architect friend, Edward Knowles, whose experience includes both public and domestic architecture—among other designs, the Wolf Trap summer concert hall, near Washington, and artist Lowell Nesbitt's stable/townhouse in Greenwich Village. The combined public and private aspects of the "house," really a tiny hamlet, intrigued Mr. Knowles. He was pleased by "a certain cadence, scale, color and a very consistent vernacular architecture." These qualities, however, needed to be emphasized. The owner had several requirements for his country home. First, he needed a place to house his collection of American folk art. He also likes to entertain, and wanted a guest house far enough from the main dwelling to ensure privacy. He gives parties that flow from space to space, starting with drinks in the living room, then dinner in the kitchen/dining area, coffee in the orangery—carved from one end of the greenhouse—and a nightcap in the icehouse/guest house.

Mr. Knowles restored the buildings by using old materials such as barn siding, weathered masonry, and floors from an old schoolhouse, along with timber from the mountain. From the timber he made rough-hewn supports that allude to Japanese tokonoma posts, designed to call attention to the surrounding smoothness. The mix of old and new materials is so skillful that it is difficult to be sure which is which. This pleasant ambiguity is continued in the space itself, which never leads precisely where it seems to be going. The original building was "superficially rational, but totally disorganized," the architect says, "with the major supports not where they should be." Rather than correct this waywardness, he capitalized on it—creating a space that is agreeably eccentric and highly functional. The collection of wooden decoys, weather vanes and handpainted nineteenth-century game boards seems to have been created expressly for the weathered wood-and-stone walls that now frame them.

The ensemble of living spaces is a typical embodiment of Mr. Knowles's theories—or, rather, his rejection of theory. He has disavowed his Bauhaus-oriented training, and once wrote: "Historical references, popular idioms, avant-garde statements, sculptural and painterly concepts all have a potential role in the design of buildings. Any academic approach to architecture is arbitrary and limiting. We are in an era that is a tornado of ideas. Our architecture should be no less." And indeed the architect has created a "tornado of ideas" with this odd but superbly convincing assortment of dwelling spaces in New York State. It is a small and quite felicitous tornado—but a forceful one nonetheless.

PRECEDING PAGE: *Architect Edward Knowles has given new life to a complex of weathered 19th-century farm buildings set on a plateau in the Hudson River Valley. Nestling at the edge of a pond are, from left to right, the greenhouse/ orangery, main house and guest house.* LEFT: *In the main house, differing floor levels demarcate the kitchen/dining area from the fire-warmed Living Room. Intriguing objects include a New Bedford whale weather vane and an American Indian whirligig on a Laotian drum.* ABOVE: *The entrance to the greenhouse/orangery—a restored Lord & Burnham structure—retains its antique delicacy.*

ABOVE: *Defined by aged vertical siding, the guest house—a former icehouse—at once preserves and adapts rural architecture.* RIGHT: *The amusing Victorian spiral stairway in the guest house leads to a sleeping balcony enlivened with Japanese calligraphy; kitchen appliances unobtrusively line the alcove beneath it. A rather formal grouping of Chinese furniture emphasizes the simplicity of the architecture. At the right is an American eagle ship's figurehead.*

Dense woods surround the unusual estate, providing both seclusion and pastoral beauty. Much of the material used in the renovation was recycled from other old buildings in the area.

SOUTHERN CALIFORNIA SERENITY

The valley is spread out in a patchwork of white fences in the middle of which is a yellow and white farm complex where the greenery of trees forms a lace edging about the main house. The compound might be in New England, but actually it is not far from Los Angeles—the 1200-acre country retreat and working ranch of Mr. and Mrs. David H. Murdock. White iron gates open to a long road leading to the main house—a road that seems almost like a covered bridge, with hundreds of oak trees forming the roof. The approach is broken by a wooden bridge that spans a pond lying in front of the jonquil-toned clapboard complex. On the quasi-antebellum veranda, pots of festively colored flowers spill over to the brick floor and walkways leading to other buildings. Beyond, the light green pastures darken to the green of the hills and the deep violet of the mountains in the distance. Prize Santa Gertrudis cattle graze near a pond on which floats a solitary duck.

"We looked for three years before we found this ranch," explains Gabriele Murdock, who acted as her own interior designer. "Because of its isolated location, I think there's nothing to indicate that you're in southern California—or even in America, for that matter." The expansive grazing lands are seen from the living room of the main house, and it is almost impossible to determine where the gardens stop and the pasture begins. "When I first saw the living room, which spans the width of the house, it was one big space. I immediately decided to divide it into two seating areas, and I feel it gives a more comfortable effect. Cozy without being cramped." Its light-hued walls are hung with a number of nineteenth-century American paintings, and the commodious chairs and sofas are upholstered in a floral fabric. "Buying the ranch opened up a whole new world for me," continues Mrs. Murdock. "Be-

fore this time I knew very little about Americana, and I was attached to English pieces. Our other homes are very traditional—English and rather conservative, with a restrained feeling about them. Here, however, I simply let my imagination go. It took approximately eight months to restore the house to the point where we were able to live in it. At the same time, of course, construction was being done on the games house and the barns, but luckily nothing had to be done to the guest house."

The finished home is as fresh as the countryside that surrounds it. The dining room is replete with Early American-style oak dining table and chairs, and complementary side tables further balance the room. Warm wood tones enhance the space, with its background of blue and white—colors repeated in the Italian tile fireplace. Directly off the living room is the master bedroom, where the predominant floral motif is set off by geometrically patterned carpeting. Opposite a decorative white fireplace, the oak canopy bed is draped in white lace. Multipaned windows abound on two sides, allowing the serene beauty of the countryside to enter the room. A collection of quilts and framed quilt remnants are the focus of the guest room. Set against a blue Chinese wallcovering, they glow with an array of reds and maroons, allowing these warm colors to wash over the Early American oak furniture.

"Initially, we were going to live in the games house and tear this house down," Gabriele Murdock recalls. "We decided against it, however, one of the reasons being that a separate guest house allowed both our guests and ourselves privacy. Another reason is that the old house was just too charming to resist." In an age of so much slick and conventional design, it is a pleasure to find a personal style executed with so much love and such a skilled hand.

Gabriele Murdock conceived interiors of warmth and elegance for her family's retreat on a 1200-acre working ranch in southern California. PRECEDING PAGE: *Eucalyptus, ash and oak trees dapple the approach to the main house, which is flanked by a games house and a pool pavilion.* RIGHT: *A placid azure pool and native California plantings introduce the long, low main house.*

RIGHT: *Against a screen of trees, the lake mirrors a wooden footbridge that connects the shore and a tranquil island.* OPPOSITE: *Corral fencing and stately trees give a processional aspect to the drive leading to the residence.*

70

LEFT: *In the Living Room, Early American and 18th-century English appointments and Chinese Export porcelain objects create a recurrent yet ever-varied theme. An antique table stands between a pair of sofas, dividing the room into two comfortable seating areas. Among the animal sculptures that grace the setting is a Mène bronze rooster, atop the table in the foreground.* ABOVE: *A framed patchwork quilt repeats the dominant colors of the room. Another Mène bronze is on the sideboard.*

ABOVE: *A tricolor palette and sturdy ladder-back chairs infuse the Dining Room with a Colonial character, enhanced by a brass chandelier and tiled fireplace. Above the mantel is an English landscape.* RIGHT: *A cheerful bower with a sunny alcove seating arrangement, the Master Bedroom presents a friendly array of sprightly checked and floral fabrics underscored by carpeting in a serrated geometric pattern.*

SCOTTISH FISHING LODGE

"It looked so like a matchbox, sitting on its green knoll. That was my first impression of the house, and we've kept it that way," says Penny Govett of the Norwegian log house her husband's family built in Scotland twenty-four years ago. Interior designer John Stefanidis has made this fishing lodge more comfortable, and prettier, too, and has banished the usual Spartan implications of other log houses.

"My husband's parents were avid fishermen," explains Mrs. Govett, "and they once had a similar house in Norway. They wanted to re-create the same house on a stretch they already owned in Scotland, on the Dee." So Norwegian craftsmen duplicated the old house log for log in an adjacent field in Norway. Each log was numbered as it went into place; the roof was raised, then taken down again, and the walls followed. Workmen put it all, and themselves, on a coal boat heading across the North Sea. In Scotland they reassembled the house on the new site, overlooking one of the best fishing pools in the area. The numbers can still be seen on the logs, and marks from the studs of the boatmen's boots still bear traces of coal dust. Time and weather have softened the exterior of the lodge, but little else has changed. The alterations made by John Stefanidis have been more in the nature of simple evolution.

Some of the most important changes involved comforts like heating and rewiring and plenty of hot water. These improvements cannot be seen, but they are more than welcome on a cold morning in the Highlands. Other additions—cupboards and specially designed furniture—are pine, complementing the walls. "If a house has a certain atmosphere, you have to be very careful not to lose that atmosphere for the sake of decoration," explains Mrs. Govett. "It's a great mistake when people throw out things that have been dear to others.

When our older generation returns for a visit, I hope they find all the familiar bits, perhaps in different places, but here somewhere. A lacquered clock, for instance, has always been around, and the house wouldn't look the same without it. Each generation should add to a house like this, and nothing should be taken away unless it is worn out." The trellised front door and a staircase with flat, jigsawed balustrades are traditional Scandinavian decorations and are still in their accustomed places. Paintings of record-size fish hang near the stairway, evoking memories of some that "didn't get away."

The Govett children are a fourth generation of enthusiastic fishermen and the keenest of all when the season starts on February 1. They wait only for the ice, or *grue*, to disappear from the river—concerned for their fishing lines, not cold toes. At midsummer, when days are long, they are likely to dine early, then continue fishing until after eleven, when long evening shadows finally darken to night. During the winter the days are short, and the family appreciates the indoor life, coming in to be warm and cozy after long walks. In the spring and summer the riverbanks are knee-deep in wild flowers, from the earliest anemones, primroses, cowslips and daisies to the lupine and rosebay willow herb of summer. Mrs. Govett gathers them as she walks along the banks to fish. In April the petals from single-flowered cherries fill the air like a spring wedding, and the garden is bright with scented narcissus. It is not an extensive garden, simply a well-ordered surround for the house. Grass and trees and bulbs are the essentials; bottle-green forests are the background. At one time there was a rose bed, but it looked inappropriate, for this is not a place for elaborate gardening. It is a place for serious fishing —and for a comfortable matchbox of a log house.

PRECEDING PAGE: *John Stefanidis hewed to the unaffected spirit of a Norwegian log house in his design for the Govett family's fishing lodge in the Scottish Highlands next to the river Dee.*

TOP LEFT: *Traditional jigsawed balustrades on the stairway in the Hall recall the Scandinavian lineage of the home.* TOP RIGHT: *A lacquered chinoiserie clock stands in the Hall, while antique wicker stretchers for wading boots indicate the entrance to the tackle room.* ABOVE AND RIGHT: *In the Sitting Room, as elsewhere, comfortable furnishings in restful neutral hues maintain the air of simplicity. The grouping of aquatints is by Graham Sutherland.*

BELOW: *In the Tackle Room, well-wrought shelves hold rods and reels; wines are stored in built-in bins. Functional cork tiles are used for flooring.* RIGHT: *A series of Henry Moore etchings in the Dining Room attests to the Yorkshire artist's fondness for sheep. Animal images are also found in the fabric covering the dining table and chairs, a subtle cotton print of tiny fishes. The landscape is by Edward Burra.*

LEFT: *In the Master Bedroom, crisp draperies enclose the pine four-poster bed; a wool rug adds warmth. A 17th-century walnut table and Russian country chairs contribute a note of gentle refinement to the rustic setting.* ABOVE: *Situated on a green knoll beside the river, the log structure is a replica of the family's lodge in Norway.*

ELIZABETHAN MANOR HOUSE

When Janet Shand Kydd first saw *Morley Old Hall*, the house slumbered at the end of a drive across flat English fields. Its only inhabitants were Muscovy ducks swimming the moat; its only gardens, primroses blooming on the banks. The house, however, had a dignity that even abandonment could not conceal. It was to be auctioned in only five days, but she needed no time to make up her mind. She bought it. Now the fields are a plantation of poplars, and the drive is lined with chestnut trees. The ducks still swim, the primroses still bloom and the manor house has come alive with all its former vigor.

The house has survived 400 years of fashionable whims without any violent stylistic changes to the exterior. No one has wrapped it in a later façade; no one has added a portico to make it grand, or torn down a wing to make it cozy. It was something of a close thing, however, and Mrs. Shand Kydd recalls a picnic at the house the day she bought it. "I had been caught up in a ridiculous bicycle race and was a bit late. By the time I got to the house all my friends had decided what they thought I should do with it. One said, 'Turn it round the other way.' Another said, 'Tear half of it down.' A third said, 'Change the windows to doors.' The only person who kept quiet was David Mlinaric, who advises the National Trust on historic houses. He stood to one side until everyone else had left and then offered his few words. 'Don't do anything. Just live in it. Then you'll know.' That was the best advice I've ever had. Norman Scarfe, an expert on English architecture, was helpful, too. He said I mustn't be tempted to add windows to the staircase, for the whole point was to have a dark transition from one very light space to another. So after listening to them, I scrapped all thoughts of change and decided to leave the architecture of the house just as it has always been."

Opinions on the date of the house differ by as much as a century, but if the stepped gables are any indication, it could be late Elizabethan. The U-shaped plan retains much of what was traditional in that time. The hall is in the center, but the simple staircase looks back to the Tudor era rather than forward in time. It is a comfortable manor house, not a stately home, and sits on its moated island much as a rough-cut stone might rest on a cushion.

Everywhere the scale is grand. Soup ladles are ten inches across, and tables ten feet long; draperies sweep generously onto the floor; bowls of potpourri are over two feet across; even books seem to be thicker and stacked higher than in other houses. The gardens are planted so luxuriantly that they appear enormous, when in fact the Anglo-Saxon moat contains them quite snugly. Gray paving stones are set in a scalloped pattern for the front courtyard, and within these there are two squares of white flowers—old-fashioned roses, peonies and poppies—each pinned at the corners with a spike of evergreen. More roses, and clematis too, spill over the moat wall like fine lace set out to dry in the sun. At the back of the house one broad path bisects the flat lawn, and on either side flower beds fifteen feet wide are crammed with an extravagant profusion of roses that tumble out across the path or soar another fifteen feet high. Yew hedges mark out a stalwart geometry that does its best to confine the glorious abundance. Again, it is a simple plan and has that enviable quality in garden design of looking inevitable. There are plans for a bridge over the moat at the back and a path through the woodlands to a secret garden enclosed by the barn and stables, but Janet Shand Kydd will add no more to what is planted there. She knows how to take the bold stroke; she also knows exactly when to stop.

Enduring dignity marks Morley Old Hall, Janet Shand Kydd's late-Elizabethan manor house in the English countryside. PRECEDING PAGE: Built around 1580, the home reflects varied architectural influences, seen in its original façade of Tudor brick, classical pediments crowning the windows, and stepped gables. The moat dates to Anglo-Saxon times. ABOVE: In the Entrance Hall, Victorian paintings grace the doorway wall; a Khmer torso stands on a window ledge. A framed fragment of 19th-century Chinese wallpaper rests against a chair. LEFT: Beneath mullioned windows in the Drawing Room, a George II agate-top table exhibits an array of objects, including a Khmer stone head. The small model of the manor is by Jill Laurimore. The allegorical paintings are by Dünz.

RIGHT: *Beams lightened with lime define the half-timbered walls of the Tudor staircase.*
BELOW RIGHT: *In the Upstairs Sitting Room, Chinese lacquered screens form an arresting background for an Italian cupboard. Sickert's* La Hollandaise *surmounts a doorway framing an Elizabethan portrait; the Charles X folio holder contains engravings.* FAR RIGHT: *In contrast to the lightness of a faux-bamboo settee, floral patterns and cheval glass in the Master Bedroom, the French armoire exemplifies Mrs. Shand Kydd's use of large-scale appointments.*

HUDSON VALLEY HAVEN

Owning a country retreat has become an almost universal fantasy in our urbanized society. All of us at one time or another have entertained the idea of withdrawing from the demands and the competition of city life and making a new beginning in some attractive slice of landscape. David Whitcomb has had the good fortune—and perhaps the good sense—to turn this usually much-postponed dream into reality at a relatively young age. As an interior designer with a flourishing New York practice, Mr. Whitcomb is a little more mobile than many. After all, a sense of color and proportion is a distinctly mobile commodity. And these qualities are more than apparent in the converted millhouse and ancillary structures that Mr. Whitcomb has turned into his year-round home near Germantown, New York. Although only a hundred miles from Manhattan, this corner of the Hudson Valley retains the imprint of 300 years of placid and commodious living.

The slow and patient assembling of his harmonious retreat began about two decades ago for David Whitcomb. That was when he first saw what was a wooden mill in rather parlous condition, a structure still owned by the Livingstons, the original lords of the manor under grants made by the English Crown over three centuries previously. Initially conceiving it as an occasional haven, the designer concentrated on turning the millhouse into an intimate and congenial summer base. Wooden walls were replaced by fieldstone, garnered from the masonry walls that are traditional in the region. The original three levels were kept, as were the wood-beamed ceilings. In order to create a Japanese-style soaking pool, the designer diverted the stream that formerly activated both the waterwheel on the outside of the millhouse and the one on·its lower level; however, the mill wheels remain entirely intact.

When Mr. Whitcomb decided to give up his New York apartment and turn his country house into a year-round residence, it was clear that enlargements had to be considered. Rather than destroy the integrity of the original building, he built an entirely new form on the landscape. It is a large, suavely shaped stainless-steel rectangle, poised like an elegant sentinel of the future at the edge of the courtyard garden, and is connected to the old house by a discreet covered passage. "One of the main reasons for my settling down full-time in the country was to pursue my love of music," explains Mr. Whitcomb. To this end, the new structure is largely given over to a single airy space, which the designer calls his studio. There is a piano, of course, and the bleached-oak floor and light fabric wallcoverings that are hallmarks of the Whitcomb sensibility. The openness of the space allows the winter sun to flood the studio, while the summer light barely comes in at all.

The millhouse, by contrast, is a warm honeycomb of tradition. Small, intimate rooms on three levels are redolent of the carefully considered and limited, but never confined, life of the Hudson Valley in 1800, the year the millhouse was built. All the pleasures of the time are here—books, good food and conversation. And in the dining room, candlelight. "It is something of a time warp," admits David Whitcomb. "Yet it is a way of life that makes demands upon you as an individual. Either you are stimulated into a deeper knowledge of yourself, or you are defeated by it. To me the country means repose, time to read and a place for my music." Making a successful transition into a more relaxed world is never easy, especially for an achieving person, but David Whitcomb seems to have mastered that transition, and his lively, evocative house is the ever-evolving and ever-growing progeny of the change.

PRECEDING PAGE: *Traditional and modern architecture meet in congenial juxtaposition in designer David Whitcomb's nearly 200-year-old millhouse and modern studio.* LEFT: *Robust rough-hewn beams frame the approach to the Dining Room, which is tucked into the lowest of the three levels of the stone millhouse. Here, a massive interior water wheel, once functional, serves as a bold design element. Hexagonal terra-cotta tiles honeycomb the floor.*

*Post-and-beam pragmatism becomes
a decorative statement in the Dining
Room, with its glowing hearth, wax
tapers and gleaming tablesettings. Armchairs, upholstered in leather and backed
with a linen plaid, ring an oval dining
table of unexpected provenance—old
barn flooring that has been bleached
and rubbed to its rightful luster.*

In the Studio, amid pastoral views, the designer can pursue his love of music. Behind the concert grand piano, a formidable wood form originally used in sand casting creates shadow play on walls textured by pandanus fiber. An antique sled chair rests on the bleached-oak flooring. The wooden figure of a child adorns a wall in the background.

In another corner of the Studio, a narrow window reveals ridges in the metal mill wheel. George Tooker's painting The Guitar *sets a romantic mood. The oil-on-canvas screen is by Durkee.*

In the Master Bedroom, unbleached
muslin drapes the iron canopy bed. Over
the fireplace is a poster illustrated with
an imperial Roman profile. A gilded
tôle church steeple stands nearby.

ABOVE: *A flower-strewn meadow surrounds the Hudson Valley retreat.* OPPOSITE: *The grape arbor provides a view of exuberant blossoms.*

CLASSIC SUMMER COTTAGE

It was eight o'clock on a gray morning when Harry Hinson caught his first glimpse of the house that has occupied so much of his attention for the past three years. "There it was, nestled at the edge of a golf course in East Hampton, looking like some rather improbable stage set. Naturally it was love at first sight." Subsequently Mr. Hinson discovered that the house had in fact been inspired by an opera. "The original owner became enamored of the little room from which the heroine in *Martha* escapes—and asked his architect to design a house around it," he explains. "I'm sure the poor man winced at the prospect, but all things considered, I think he emerged with a good deal of credit." It is a long way, architecturally and historically, from 1919 and the taste of that era for half-timbering and the discreet Tudor references that the house embodies. Perhaps it has something to do with the turning wheel of fashion, but the well-mannered elevations of Mr. Hinson's country retreat manage to look charming without being too sentimental or too claustrophobic.

"I have a theory about quality," says Mr. Hinson. "If an object—or a piece of furniture or a house—sets out to do its job in an unaffected manner, then I think it's bound to succeed. In this case all the architect ever intended was to design an unpretentious cottage to serve as an adjunct to the rather enormous house nearby, a place the original owners could come to in the winter. Now it provides me with a refuge from the frantic pace of city life."

Mr. Hinson found the house furnished. It had been taken care of proficiently over the years but not "feelingly," as he puts it. His first priority was to eliminate most of the furniture, but no significant structural changes were made. And there were delightful idiosyncrasies to explore—ceilings that range from twelve feet in the living room down to seven in the dining room, and a generous fireplace with its own half-timbered detailing. Basically the house was an appealing blank, waiting for the hands of a skillful colorist to give it life and breadth.

The way people tacitly divide their lives according to the changing seasons rather annoys Mr. Hinson. "I never was a seasonal slipcover person. It's absurd to think of an interior as being absolutely restricted by the months of the year you might wish to spend in it. People tend to associate summer with light fabrics such as linens and bleached colors, and winter with a sense of coziness, sometimes so intense it becomes positively overwhelming. But life really takes place between these extremes." An avoidance of polarization, then, is one way to describe the house. And yet the middle ground that Mr. Hinson has colonized is not a bland place: "I've done things that were mildly eccentric, I think—such as cutting down my old office desk and using it as a table. I'm very proud of it and invariably point it out."

Simplicity is the word that keeps recurring as the house is discovered. "It takes a great deal of complexity to arrive at something that is ultimately pared down," says Harry Hinson. "This house is now really very much a solution arrived at by subtraction. I feel it reflects a mature sensibility." A gentle and rather vivacious sense of style also describes Mr. Hinson's approach. Being the sort of person he is—a man with a talent to amuse and instruct—it is not surprising that both his business interests and his home reflect the same qualities. The most important thing? "Perhaps to be interested in the absurd as well as the sublime," says Harry Hinson with a characteristic half-smile. His house manages to reflect neither of these extremes, however, but rather to be situated in that satisfying middle ground to which so many aspire with less success.

PRECEDING PAGE: *Designer Harry Hinson's retreat from the confines of Manhattan is a seaside Tudor-style lodge in East Hampton.*

RIGHT: *Linen drapery and seating fabrics complement the period atmosphere of the Living Room, which is enhanced by a bountiful provincial-style fireplace. A gilded ram's head is poised over a doorway. The engraving is by Albrecht Dürer.*

Mr. Hinson prefers informality for his country house—not "masked balls on the lawn." Spatter-patterned fabric that gives the appearance of rough plaster promotes an Early American quality in the Dining Room. An antique silver Guernsey pitcher atop a washed-pine bar, and a braided rug, contribute to the feeling of country ease.

TOP: *The effect of cotton is crisp in an upstairs Bedroom appointed with a washed-pine campaign chest and chair.*
ABOVE: *Geometric-patterned cotton fabric defines another Bedroom.*

An interplay of light and dark hues distinguishes the Master Bedroom, where deep-toned walls counterpoint pristine cotton and silk fabrics. Lilies soften the precision with their foliage.

NEW ENGLAND FARMHOUSE

There was a time when few successful New York interior designers in search of a country place of their own would have been tempted by an American-Victorian farmhouse, however unspoiled its setting. But now Keith Irvine's choice of such a house in New England seems almost classic. The British-born decorator made his choice more than fifteen years ago and, characteristically, he was less concerned with being a trend-setter than with acquiring a home mellowed by age, but not so inhibitingly historic that it called for reverential treatment. He intended it as a rural retreat for himself, his wife, Chippy, and their two young daughters. Gradually it has become a year-round residence. In addition, the barn has been turned into an alternative house where the Irvines spend the summer. It is a seasonal move of a hundred yards that gives them a pleasant change without the upheaval of an annual vacation.

Rehabilitation and refurnishing over the last ten years have been a combined family effort. "We did everything ourselves," Mr. Irvine says, "except the electrical work and the plumbing." A small part of the farmhouse dates from 1790, but the rest is a typical 1870s construction, with relatively large rooms and well suited to the kind of decoration—handsome but lighthearted, gently ironic while genuinely comfortable—that is second nature to Keith Irvine. "I have always kept close to what I admired when I was a schoolboy; 1840 was my 'moment,' then as now—the Lord Melbourne period, roughly everything from Regency to mid-Victorian."

Though he is unwilling to take himself too seriously, it would be wrong to assume that this designer is an amiable joker unfairly endowed with talent. One of the reasons for his success is that he knows the rudiments and refinements of his profession so thoroughly that he is able to be somewhat casual about them. As a young Scot in England in the 1950s, he had the good fortune, and the ability, to serve for four years as assistant to one of the outstanding masters of twentieth-century interior design, the late John Fowler. Some of the most cherished pieces in his farmhouse today were bequeathed to him by his famous mentor, and in Keith Irvine's own home, where he has naturally been free to indulge his personal tastes, there is undeniably much that is pleasantly evocative of the decorative technique in which John Fowler excelled.

As in the work of Fowler, so in the work of Irvine. It is rather easier to list the ingredients than to describe the dish. Superlative English furniture and carefully oiled and preserved leather-bound books, many flowered chintzes, needlework rugs, animal portraits, quilts a touch of tartan and a twist of Gothic—all play their memorable roles in the interior of the Irvine farmhouse. But so too do innumerable less predictable elements: an Edwardian Chippendale-style table, the throne on which Vivien Leigh sat when she played Cleopatra, a portrait of Mr. Irvine in his youth, wittily disguised as Mary, Queen of Scots. "I like mixing 1920s and 1930s American rattan with very good classical pieces, and Staffordshire china with Chinese Export porcelain," says Keith Irvine. "For me, Staffordshire has a certain *literary* quality that I love." The same might be said about his own decorative idiom, which has sometimes been called the "English country house" style. All well and good, provided you admit it is as valid in America as in England, and do not confuse "country house" with "stately home." It has nothing to do with guided tours and misguided paying guests—but a lot to do with sound education and a sense of humor, with wood fires and open windows, with buttered toast for tea, with children and dogs.

The country atmosphere of an 1870s Victorian
farmhouse in New England is the result of renovation by designer Keith Irvine and his family.
PRECEDING PAGE: The colonnaded front portico
adds distinction to the structure. ABOVE: Local
stone, rough-hewn beams and a raffia rug give
rustic appeal to the Dining Room. A mid-
Victorian Scottish portrait of a boy evokes the
period during which the house was built.

Enhancing the traditional look of the Dining Room is a folding screen covered with early-19th-century wallpaper panels by Swiss designer Jean Zuber; the panels depict English monarchs Henry VIII and Elizabeth I. Antique Irish walnut dining chairs surround a table invitingly set with an 18th-century porcelain dinner service.

111

The Sitting Room décor projects a
literary quality. A watercolor of a
tree-shaded cottage, by A. C. Bowen,
two early-19th-century equestrian
studies and other small artworks lend
a rural theme. The 18th-century
Hepplewhite armchair is upholstered
in an appropriate pastoral print.

Cherished photographs and furnishings generate a familial ambience in the Master Bedroom. A 17th-century Chinese armchair rests at the foot of a canopy bed covered with a 19th-century American quilt. A Victorian child's wing chair is underscored by the 18th-century English needlepoint rug.

113

An American mahogany canopy bed dating from 1860 dominates another Bedroom, providing an anchor for the gaiety of Victorian document wallpaper. Edwardian lace boudoir pillows complement bedside table drapery fashioned from a Victorian lace dress.

A profusion of vintage dolls mingles cheerfully with contemporary toys in a child's Bedroom. A delicate muslin, fancifully draped above a 19th-century American bed, combines with sheer draperies and pinstripe wallpaper to create a light and airy setting.

NEAR SAINT-TROPEZ

Unlike today, the Côte d'Azur of the nineteenth century was a seaside resort most popular in the winter months. The era, it must be remembered, was one in which ladies avoided the sun in order to preserve their pale and delicate complexions. So in winter the wealthy came to the south of France from every part of the world, escaping either the climate or the turmoil—or both—of their native lands. They built immense Baroque villas, and with them came the polished adventurers and adventuresses who flitted through the new palaces and casinos. At the time, Saint-Tropez was still a modest fishing village, far removed from this involved and glamorous way of life. Discovered by the painter Signac in 1872, it was destined to be an artists' colony before becoming a fashionable seaside resort.

After World War II more and more people crowded into Saint-Tropez—at first, the existentialists of Saint-Germain-des-Prés in Paris, then the followers of Françoise Sagan and Roger Vadim and Brigitte Bardot. Today, the quais of the port resemble a giant fairground. For thousands the simple fishing village has become a magical place where they can see film stars and other celebrities at their most informal. The wheel, however, is beginning to come full circle, for those who truly love the old image of Saint-Tropez are avoiding the present-day port and its crowded beaches. They close down their houses in August, returning in the fall to the rhythms of another age, to the off-seasons, when they can enjoy the natural beauty around them that the summer emphasis on sun and ocean tends to obscure.

In such a spirit one Parisian, an art collector, began searching for a home in the vicinity of Saint-Tropez but sufficiently removed from its contemporary bustle. He soon fell in love with a twelfth-century house in a rural landscape rich with vineyards and olive trees and eucalyptus. Formerly part of a Medieval complex, the house had been built with care, and complemented its site in every way. Previous owners, however, had pointed up its "rustic" nature by multiplying the small-paned windows, drawing false tiles in the cement and uncovering the old beamed ceilings. The garden itself had been provided with an imitation well and strewn with carefully disorganized piles of brush. The new resident wanted none of this. He sought something "more severe and more consistent with the origins of the dwelling."

Consequently he called upon interior designer Daniel Kiener to simplify the house and open it up to the surrounding landscape. M. Kiener was given carte blanche to add a wing, design new furniture, build a swimming pool and rearrange the garden. In the new wing he installed a dressing room for the swimming pool, a garage and a salon d'été, a summer living room. Here, the small-paned windows were replaced by large arches with sliding glass doors that can be made to magically disappear from sight.

The same natural simplification has been given to the form and structure of the interior of the house. Walls and floors are white, cupboards and closets are built-in, and there are many pieces of contemporary furniture, both functional and comfortable, designed by M. Kiener himself. The décor is cool and immaculate, here and there dramatically animated by Chinese red lacquer, a patchwork quilt in tones of blue, and canvases by contemporary French artists of the Supports/Surfaces group. The paintings themselves are discreet, underscoring the simple and austere setting by avoiding any theatrical or ostentatious effects. In fact, with such art on the walls of his country house, the owner has reaffirmed the proud traditions of Saint-Tropez that equate the love of light with the love of painting.

*In updating a 12th-century farmhouse near Saint-Tropez,
designer Daniel Kiener favored a theme of pristine and
spare simplicity.* PRECEDING PAGE: *Deep-set windows and
the patina of roof tiles embellish the sturdy structure, while
trees and flowers soften its contours.* BELOW: *The Salon
d'Hiver reflects a harmony of tone and texture. Doorways
flanking the fireplace lead to the salon d'été.* OPPOSITE AND
OPPOSITE BELOW: *The Salon d'Eté functions as a breeze-
way: Arches with glass doors that slide away into the walls
open the room to the elements. The painting above the bar
table is by Louis Cane; the shaped painting is by Dezeuze.*

118

119

The arch motif recurs in the Dining Room, where a vaulted
ceiling recalls the Medieval origin of the structure.
A woolen rug offsets the lacquered brilliance of a bamboo
dining table and chairs, and a large arched storage cabinet.

A glass wall in the Master Bedroom superimposes reflections on a view of the platform-elevated Bath. The dark Louis Cane painting is apprehended directly, while a repeat painting by Viala is seen through a glass, brightly.

HORSTED PLACE

"Victorian architecture is rather coarse, so it is not always easy to find the right furniture to place against it. The pieces must be large." Lady Rupert Nevill is talking about *Horsted Place*, her English country house. "It is the same with the patterns one chooses for the wallpapers. They have to be bold." The present owners moved here from *Uckfield House*, three miles away, some years ago. The substantial mansion was built in 1851 by a Francis Barchard, from his inherited fortune. His specifications rejected many adornments of the period, but he required, nevertheless, an imposing residence with spacious rooms and large windows. The ground floor corridor runs the length of the house. It is repeated on the same scale on the bedroom floor above, and the bold effect is echoed outside, where the view stretches south across the Sussex Downs.

The impression of the mansion, after the approach through a drive of trees, is of a gracious, friendly house on a scale both large and unpretentious. This is achieved through Lady Rupert's style and determination, the many family possessions, and the professional advice that was sought for garden plans and the arrangement of the décor. Interior designer Carl Toms was called in to collaborate on the interior. He restyled the library, and in Lady Rupert's bathroom he painted the walls with flowers, simulating china. Singularly elegant is the effect here of tall windows curtained in old cream-colored lace. Many of the wallpapers were created by the artist and Art Nouveau expert Martin Battersby.

Lord Rupert Nevill is private secretary to the duke of Edinburgh, and his London residence is a grace-and-favor apartment in St. James's Palace. Lady Rupert, however, particularly loves the Sussex country house, for its many pleasing associations. Some of these memories are evoked by a mixture of possessions, scents and sounds. Looking coolly efficient, adding another log to the library fire, she appears far from sentimental. Yet she speaks gently and nostalgically: "The house and garden remind me of my childhood home and of my happy beginnings. The smell of box, when rained upon or warm from the sun; magnolia and beeswax; potpourris; blue-bottles buzzing against a windowpane." And she adds, smiling: "The completely pure early childhood smell of certain soaps and scrubbed wooden bathtubs." She is a passionate gardener. Many of the trees, shrubs and plants in the garden—landscaped by Geoffrey Jellicoe—came from the old house. And, exactly as the house has many ties with family and friends, so does the garden. Rooted cuttings came from the gardens of friends, and there are violets that first grew in the garden at *Sissinghurst*. Lady Rupert Nevill applies concentrated thought to minute details. What she retained from the original property and what she has added as present owner are in perfect harmony. For instance, the entrance hall has paved Minton encaustic tiles, but the inner courtyard garden has new tiles keyed to the bright blue of a mosaic she saw and admired in Iran.

Perhaps the most dramatic change concerns the main staircase—originally designed by Pugin—a portion of which was exhibited in the Medieval Court of the Great Exhibition in 1851. Now painted white, it banishes any Victorian heaviness, but plays upon the fantasy of the Gothic mood. Heraldic birds carved on the newel posts of the stairs represent the Barchard crest. Eaglelike, they are somewhat stern, but definitely reassuring. Like the family who live here—and the manner in which guests are made to feel welcome—these birds are thoroughly at home. They look as if they have known many changes and fully approve of what they see today.

PRECEDING PAGE: *Rose-covered iron arches shade a slate-paved path leading to Horsted Place, the Sussex country home of Lord and Lady Rupert Nevill. The fanciful chimneys and gables of the 1851 diapered brick structure create a picturesque background.*

BELOW: *The oak staircase, which was designed by Pugin, is now freshened and lightened with paint.* RIGHT: *A Hepplewhite child's chair stands at the draped doorway that connects the two areas of the double Drawing Room. Garden flowers and a cheerful floral chintz printed from old pattern blocks add to the informal appeal of the room.*

RIGHT: *A mirrored panel in the Drawing Room provides a background for a Victorian papier-mâché lamp atop an 18th-century Dutch walnut commode. A French botanical watercolor completes the composition.*

RIGHT: *An inviting corner of the Drawing Room is appointed with a French writing table and an antique bellpull. The portrait is 17th-century English.*

In the Drawing Room, commodious
seating blends with mahogany pieces,
Chinese porcelain vases mounted as
lamps, and family photographs.

Sir John Hoppner's ancestral portrait of Urania, Countess of Portsmouth, dominates the Dining Room. Early-Georgian silhouettes of members of Lord Rupert Nevill's family face the portrait. The Victorian Gothic dining chairs were brought from Eridge Castle, Lord Rupert's family seat.

ABOVE LEFT: *Gothic-style dark wood moldings in the Library frame bookcases, cabinets and art. The Thornhill portrait of Isaac Newton is a focal point.* LEFT: *The octagonal shape of Lady Rupert's Bedroom allows for a bed alcove and several walk-in closets. A favorite gown has been reinterpreted as a skirt for the dressing table.*

CLOSEBURN STUD

"I didn't choose the house," confesses Mrs. C. Cannon Cogswell, "the house chose me." The house in question is a rather conventional structure set on a small hill near Millbrook, New York, and overlooking rolling countryside thick with trees. "The truth of the matter is, I bought it for the barns," she says —as well as, surely, for its 150 acres and the large indoor riding ring, stables, outbuildings and cottages that make up the horse farm *Closeburn Stud*.

Purchased from Bennett College, the farm is a chapter that fits quite logically into the story of its owner's life. Racing, showing, jumping—these have always been Mrs. Cogswell's enthusiasms. She explains: "I've lived in Millbrook since the 1930s, and we've owned Thoroughbred horses all my life." Boasting an equine population of a stallion and forty to fifty brood mares, Closeburn Stud carries on the family tradition faithfully and with Mrs. Cogswell's considerable vigor. Typical days at the horse farm are hectic ones, and during foaling season everyone stays up with the night watchman until dawn. Business often takes Mrs. Cogswell to Ireland, England and France, and horses do seem to elicit her greatest enthusiasm. There are even depictions of horse racing and the hunt in print after print in the library.

Though Mrs. Cogswell concentrates on horses, she also directed considerable attention to her home's interior, with assistance from designers Ned Marshall and Harry Schule of Marshall Schule Associates. As the process of designing the house was set in motion, it became a question of assembling disparate pieces from Mrs. Cogswell's London home and her New York apartment, "and then making them work in a new environment—getting the pieces in there," says Mr. Marshall, "and pushing them around." There were certain colors Mrs. Cogswell wanted: her favorite red, pink, turquoise

and aqua. She says: "I always keep to the same colors, because my mother said if you have roughly the same colors wherever you live, you can move them easily from country to country," something that Mrs. Cogswell, who lived in England for ten years, has had no trouble in doing. The red and white plantings around the house reflect not only her preference but also the colors of her "life silks," the colors worn by the jockeys racing her horses.

If horses are Mrs. Cogswell's first passion, interior design runs a close second. She has been an avid collector of fine furniture—primarily English and French pieces—for a good many years now, so when it came time to furnish the house, few further selections had to be made. "Her theory," Ned Marshall points out, "and ours too, is that if it's all of an approximate period, it doesn't really matter what country each piece is from." Though the quality of pieces is uniformly high, the pervading atmosphere of the house is low-key, clearly fitting for a country seat. Casual though the rooms may appear, however, life at Closeburn Stud is anything but. Hunt breakfasts, large dinners and other entertainments are features of the brisk social pace at the farm, and there are always horses. "You can be having cocktails Saturday night with Cynthia and her friends," Harry Schule explains, "and she'll be called down to the stables because a horse is foaling—the end of a typical day." These matters bother Mrs. Cogswell not in the least. Most mornings find her at her desk in the library, conferring with the farm manager; on the phone with various racetracks, breeders and trainers; planning which fillies to buy or sell, which to race, which to retain for the sake of bloodlines. "And the best part is," she points out with evident satisfaction, "I can sit at my desk in the library and see everything." Missing, of course, not a thing.

At Closeburn Stud, her horse farm near Millbrook, New York, Mrs. C. Cannon Cogswell delights in Ned Marshall's and Harry Schule's traditional design for the main house. PRECEDING PAGE: A flower-strewn hillside overlooks the large main stable. OPPOSITE: Country ease pervades the Drawing Room, in which the designers used pieces from Mrs. Cogswell's collection of predominantly 18th-century English furniture. A painting by L. Lüthy, of a mid-1800s Manhattan residence, extends the rural flavor. ABOVE: A painted niche, displaying pieces of an antique porcelain dinner service, seasons the Dining Room with exuberant color. English Chippendale chairs surround the table. The ancestral portrait is from the 19th century.

ABOVE: *A stable and paddock reflect the equine activity that is central to life at Closeburn Stud. Flower beds sport the colors of the Cogswell silks.* OPPOSITE: *A pond reflects the verdure surrounding the Colonial-style residence.*

STATELY SUSSEX HOME

Bentley has grown from a modest sixteenth-century farmhouse, just north of the South Downs, into a most unusual English country mansion. All of this has come about through the desires and experiments of its owners, Mrs. Gerald Askew and her late husband. Mary Askew has some refreshing, positive ideas about the way she likes her surroundings to be. She appreciates the classical style and a scale of living in grand manner. "My *folie de grandeur* really began when I saw some French châteaux just after World War II," she explains. "I became fascinated with Elsie de Wolfe's work, especially the gardens she had created at the Trianon Villa at Versailles. That did it. I Frenchified everything here. I'd been through all sorts of phases," she says, recalling her Tudor phase, with wooden beams everywhere.

Bentley is believed to have once been a vast house set in parkland. Traces of the original park can still be detected, and it is recorded that a house was on the site as early as the fourteenth century. Gerald Askew bought the farm property in the 1930s. He modernized it, farmed it and started the Bentley Stud, selling yearlings until his death, in 1970. In 1960 two important landmarks came about for the Askews. First, the Bentley Wildfowl Collection was born. Second, the distinguished architect, the late Raymond Erith, R.A., then rebuilding the prime minister's residence in Downing Street, was called in to build new wings. Mary Askew explains the Italian architectural influence: "By then we had decided that what we really wanted was to live in a sumptuous, sunny Italian villa. We were anxious to have that particular atmosphere and grandeur, but without moving from the rural depths of Sussex." The solution was to create a Mediterranean villa from an English farmhouse. "First, one Palladian wing was added on," Mrs. Askew recalls. "Then we

decided it must balance the front door, by now no longer in its rightful place in the middle of the house. So the second wing went on, to balance the first."

About this time Gerald Askew saw naturalist Peter Scott's wildfowl sanctuary and ordered a consignment of birds. "He simply announced that twenty pairs were going to be delivered," relates Mary Askew, with a wide grin, "but we had no arrangement for them—and no water! Miraculously we found springs here and bulldozed a wet old field into ponds." Once the Askews embarked on this task and "got our teeth into it," as Mary Askew describes their transforming of the grounds into a perfect environment for the birds, many species of rare waterfowl began their arrival procession. In a few years the collection was open to the public.

Mary Askew describes the original overall effect she wanted at Bentley as "nothing banal, no boring mahogany, everything rather crumbling, and nothing overrestored, the main pieces of furniture to be weighty and heavy—nothing at all spindly." She describes her home as a "dotty house, very round and about and up and down." In fact, everything is an integral part of the main scheme, and each object looks comfortable in its place. A pretty little white wire aviary stands empty, its door open, under a tree near the house. This cage has been there since it housed actor Dirk Bogarde's parrot. The empty cage should look a bit eccentric, yet it certainly does not.

"I came here to Bentley as a bride," says Mrs. Askew. "It has been my only home, and I've wanted to live only here. I've devoted so much energy to carrying out our ideas, and I've enjoyed making this into the place it is. So I hope it will continue. For when I plant a tree, it is not important to me that I live to stand under it. Bentley could have become a hodgepodge, but I believe it has turned out well."

136

OPPOSITE: *The Octagonal Room features an oyster-shell grotto chair, a Louis XVI chair and a painted table.*
OPPOSITE BELOW: *In the Bird Room, from left to right, are paintings of Askew family members on horseback by Molly Latham, a painting of a horse by J. Wootton, Philip Rickman's wildfowl studies and an 18th-century swan painting by Peter Casteels.* BELOW: *Norman Hepple's portrait of the late Gerald Askew is a focal point of the appropriately named Bird Room. At right are ten wildfowl paintings by Philip Rickman and a painting of a horse by J. Seymour. The center table and console with painted metal swans were made in the London workshop of O. F. Wilson.*

BELOW: *A buoyant mood pervades the Master Bedroom, where framed 18th-century fans echo the scalloped trim of a four-poster bed, inspired by one in Ireland's Birr Castle. Complementing the lighthearted décor are Regency bedside tables and an antique Aubusson rug.* OPPOSITE: *Panels of antique French wallpaper constitute a genteel vista in the Sitting Room. A Louis XVI bergère stands near an Italian daybed, which is flanked by an antique terra-cotta urn and an ornate Empire stand.* OPPOSITE BELOW: *The grounds of Bentley are a preserve for many species of waterfowl.*

RUSTIC HARMONY

"I like to create settings for something wonderful to happen in," says interior designer Paul Leonard, as he looks with satisfaction around the hospitable country living room that is the heart of his Roxbury, Connecticut house. Creating this setting has taken years, because the architectural parts that make up today's whole had to be assembled and reconstructed piecemeal, and because Mr. Leonard chose to do much of the work himself in his spare time.

The first step was finding the right site and the right structure. Only after a year-long search, ending in 1968, did he locate the living room wing of his future house. Despite the considerable state of disrepair—"ratty" is the owner's uncompromising word for it—the building seemed preordained for his purposes. "I literally gasped when I walked in here, it was so right." T'Other House, as it was known, had been built in the 1930s as a party barn by the original owners, who lived nearby in a conventional house. Barnlike in style, it stood atop a knoll within a grove of fine old ash and oak trees and looked out from its long west wall toward protected woodlands and far, rolling hills. Its interior was essentially one single room, crossed with massive 150-year-old handhewn hickory beams, and with a ceiling that peaked at eighteen feet. Its floors were random-width hickory planks, and a baronial stone fireplace and hearth gave the room a reassuring solidity.

Paul Leonard knew that he had a major job of restructuring, renovating and landscaping ahead of him, but a unique mix of professional experience—first as a theatrical designer and scenic artist, then as a kind of designer-in-residence for the Paul Mellon family and their six establishments—made the job seem easy by comparison. "I had long since learned that there are times in the design field when you have to be ready to take on just about any task, be it

wiring and plumbing, furniture designing, drapery-making, bricklaying, gardening or planning a party for a hundred. By the time I started my house, I had done it all. This was going to be fun!" He also knew that he would need more space than the original barn provided: a larger kitchen, a dining room, another bedroom or two, a couple of baths. "I thought that if I could find another barn and somehow link the two buildings together, I would really have something. I scouted around until I discovered an ancient dairy barn for sale in Bethlehem, a few miles away. I had it dismantled, loaded on a truck and brought here. When I had all the pieces lying about in the meadow, it made a formidable sight." Eagerly the new owner began building scale models of various possible arrangements, until he had what he calls "barnyard architecture" to his liking. "Hooking the two buildings together so they related organically to each other and to the land was the most challenging part of the project. What you see outside is just as important as what you see inside."

Keeping the informal character of country barns inside was important, too. "A Federal farmhouse, a Victorian house or any architectural period places some constraints upon you to furnish accordingly. But I decided I didn't want any kind of 'look.' Rather, my house was to be an amalgam of pleasing things— easy, comfortable things, things that are important to me, to my wife, Valerie, to our daughter, Samantha —so long as they all work together." Now that Paul Leonard is finished with his house, does he have any regrets? "No one is ever finished with his own place, nor should he be. A house is a living, vital thing and is always in the process of becoming, as people change. It is, in a sense, a history of you, of what you are and of what you care about. As my family and I change and grow, so our house will, too."

144

PRECEDING PAGE: *To create his informal country home in Roxbury, Connecticut, designer Paul Leonard joined together two barns: T'Other House (right), which was built in the 1930s, and a former dairy barn, which he transported to the site and reconstructed.*

ABOVE: *Connecting the structures, the Lower Hallway abounds with natural treasures and mementos set off by wood flooring and walls painted in a soft blend of hues.*
ABOVE RIGHT AND OPPOSITE: *The Living Room/Studio is crowned by 150-year-old hickory beams and brightened by casement windows. Adroit groupings define the two sections of the room. In the living area are a Louis XV-style armchair, an American bentwood chair, and a tufted sofa. The ceramic plate is by Ron Dier. A long English worktable provides the focus in the studio area. A small painting by Molyneux rests on a portable landscape easel.*

RIGHT: *In the Dining Room, the designer perpetuated the country flavor by using a combination of woods, walls covered in strié-painted canvas and subtly painted wood flooring. The collage on the mantel, a grid of leaves, is by Robert Courtright; the lucid architectonic drawing between the windows is by Richard Diebenkorn.* ABOVE: *A Louis XV-style armoire—its doors removed—displays a harmonious still life of baskets, ceramics and other unassuming objects.*

OPPOSITE AND LEFT: *In the Master Bedroom, apple matting—made by English apple pickers—establishes a comfortable, natural atmosphere. Heightening the effect are an American quilt, a handwoven throw and pillows on the 19th-century Swedish settee, and a collection of antique blue glass. Artworks include a watercolor by Shirley Oaks above the mantel and (right) drawings from Mr. Leonard's sketchbook.*

CREDITS

WRITERS

The following writers prepared the original *Architectural Digest* articles from which the material in this book has been adapted:

Helen Barnes

Peter Carlsen

Bruno de Hamel

Elizabeth Dickson

Luis Escobar

Jean-Louis Gaillemin

David Halliday

Richard Horn

Elizabeth Lambert

Valentine Lawford

Suzanne Stark Morrow

Wendy Murphy

Gerrold A. Turnbull

Carol Vogel

All original text adapted by Cameron Curtis McKinley.

All original captions adapted by Kirsten Grimstad.

PHOTOGRAPHERS

Jaime Ardiles-Arce 42–49, 100–107

Thomas S. Berntsen 130–135

Robert Emmett Bright 16–23

Emerick Bronson 60–67

Bruno de Hamel 50–59

Daniel Eifert 8-15, 90-99

Pascal Hinous 116–121

Horst 108-115

Russell MacMasters 2-7, 68-75

Derry Moore 32-41, 84-89, 112-129, 136-143

James Mortimer 76-83

José Luis Pérez 24–31

Peter Vitale 144-151

DESIGN

Design Direction:
Philip Kaplan, Executive Graphics Director
Knapp Communications Corporation

Book Design and Production:
Glen Iwasaki
B.T. Miyake Productions